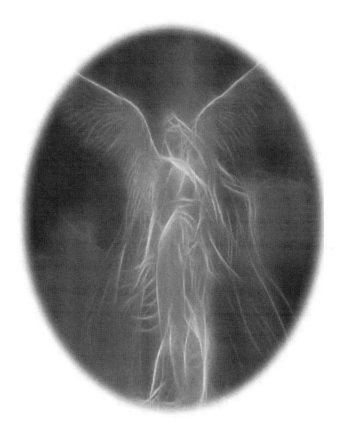

Inspired by the Holy Spirit

Written by Minister Gwendolyn Dickens Bowen

First Printing ISBN 9781974413218
Elite Publication 5324 New Hope Commons Dr. Durham, North Carolina 27707 Ordering Information: Special discounts are available on quantity purchases by corporations, associations, educators, and others. For details, contact the publisher at the above address U.S. trade bookstores and wholesalers: Please contact Jessie Bowen Tel: (919) 919-618-8075 or email elitecorporatecoaching@gmail.com.

TABLE OF CONTENTS

Dedication 4

Acknowledgement 4

About the Author...6

From My Mothers' Womb… 11

Raise up a Child... 14

But God… 15

God Prepares You...18

God Is Able…The Power of a Fervent Prayer 25

SO, WHAT IS PRAYER? 32

DAY ONE:...39

DAY TWO:...46

DAY THREE: 51

DAY FOUR:...60

DAY FIVE:...64

Calvary Covered It All… 68

When life is no more as you knew it… 77

My Soul Cries Out… 82

A Charge To Women 86

PRAY WITHOUT CEASING...92

Dedication

To my parents, Elder Joe Willie Dickens, Sr. and Mother Isabelle Knight Dickens who first introduced me to the teachings and how to live a life for Jesus Christ and my siblings (John Ivory, Brenda Faye, Josie, Melvena, Maxine, Martha, Joe, William, Robin, Jeffrey) for sharing this journey with me.

Acknowledgement

A special thank you to God, for HE has anointed and blessed me with a truer understanding of who HE is and what my Purpose is. To my husband, Jessie Bowen, for his inspiration, push and belief that I could do this. To Apostle Donnie Phillips, Sr. and the Oak Grove Christian Church Family, words cannot express my gratitude for your support and embracing me with your love and prayers. To my sister-in-law, (Pastor, Evangelist Annie Howard) who has been my Prayer Partner and Spiritual Advisor, how do I say, "thank you"?

About the Author

Minister Gwendolyn Dickens Bowen is a born-again woman of God. She received Christ at an early age during Vacation Bible School at White's Chapel Missionary Baptist Church, Speed, N.C. She was baptized in the running waters of a creek near Batts Chapel Baptist Church in Edgecombe County by the late Reverend J.E. James. As a child she didn't know what had happened, but she knew that something was different, because, when Rev. James dipped her in the name of the Father, in the name of the Son and in the name of the Holy Ghost she remembered coming up and everybody looked different. She now knows it was the presence of the Holy Spirit and she has never been the same.

She is a graduate of Fayetteville State University, majoring in Early Childhood Education. She is a retired Elementary School teacher from the Edgecombe County Public Schools System and is a Certified Life Success Coach.

She is the daughter of the late Elder Joe Willie Dickens, Sr. and Mother Isabelle Knight Dickens and is the 9th child of 11 children. She is married to Mr. Jessie Earl Bowen and through this union she has been blessed with 3 daughters, 2 sons and 13 grands.

God in His omnipotent way, saw a need to elevate Gwen's service for Him. She had felt the calling upon her life to preach the Gospel but continually found excuses as to why she shouldn't. During a service at Oak Grove Christian Church, Greenville, NC on May 11, 2016, the Prophet for the service called her out. He stated that she was being called into the ministry. It was at that moment that she openly shared that she was being called of God to preach and she accepted her calling.

Minister Bowen says she is not only thankful but grateful that God loves her so much that HE would assign her such a task. But to not only assign her but assign her helpmate as well, for he is in agreement and is always supporting her calling. He prays for and with her, he purchases materials that he feels will help advance her studies and share in conversations with her of messages he has listened to. Minister Gwen knows, God will give you just what you need.

On November 26, 2016, Minister Bowen preached her initial sermon and has been on a mission to tell dying men and women about the God she serves, reclaiming the backslider and restoring hope to the hopeless. On December 10, 2017, Minister Bowen will be Ordained.

Minister Gwen would have you to know that God has a purpose for each of our lives. It matters not who you are, who you think you are, what you're doing, what you've done, where you're going or where you've been. Fair warning, she says, "night is coming, and no man will be able to work". Don't let Him catch you with your work undone!

Jesus Loves Me

Anna B. Warner

William B. Bradbury

From My Mothers' Womb...

In the wee early morning hours of August 26, 1958, the awaited moment had arrived. Elder Joe Willie and Isabelle Knight Dickens witnessed the arrival of a promise. A promise to once again after 8 baby blessings to be blessed with a 9th blessing. This birth was different, for this was the first child to be born not by midwife but in the local "Edgecombe General Hospital" located in Tarboro, North Carolina.

There was something special about this baby, as witnessed by the delivering nurse, Martha Plemmer, whose husband Walter Plemmer would in later years become this child's music teacher. She, Martha asked if she could name the baby. Mother Dickens said yes, and she was named Gwendolyn Patricia Dickens. In years to come, Gwen asked her mom, "mom, why did you let her name me two first names?", she replied, "I told her she could name you". Gwen's dad could not pronounce "Gwendolyn" so he was the only one to call her "Grenda". And yes, she was a daddy's girl!

Everyone recognized the baby's physical beauty and she was told they reached for her. They felt a need to hold her, to be close to her. Why? Five beautiful baby girls were born before her, yet there was something different?

Could it be, because she had received the anointing while yet in her mother's womb?

~   He will love thee, and bless thee, and multiply thee; he will also bless the fruit of thy womb ~

Deuteronomy 7:13

Raise up a Child...

As a youngster, I was raised in a Christian home, not just by reading the "WORD" but being taught through daily Biblical actions. Being the ninth of eleven children, I recall being taught by a stern yet loving man of God, Elder Joe Willie Dickens, Sr. (Primitive Baptist) and a devoted wife and loving mother, Mother Isabelle Knight Dickens (Missionary Baptist).

I never remembered a discussion about their Christian denominations.

We just knew they supported each other and mom would be found getting dad's basket (food) ready for him to take for the fellowship after service. She would tell him to give it to Sis. Louvenia Lloyd to serve. Attending services with dad, I knew the words to some of the songs because they were the same in both churches but were song somewhat differently. And of course, the Baptist song with music and the Primitive Baptist song without. Yet, the meaning and that special feeling that seemingly came from my "belly" was the same. Sometimes we would choose to go with dad, but most times went with mom. This might have been because we got to see our cousins and friends.

But God…

I can remember the excitement and an eagerness to get to White's Chapel Missionary Baptist Church to hear what Rev. James had to say; to hear what the Sunday school teacher (Mrs. Ada P. Williams) had to say; or to sing the songs we had been taught in choir practice. I was baptized in the running waters of a creek near Batts Chapel Missionary Baptist Church in Edgecombe County by the late Reverend J.E.

James. As a child I didn't know what had happened, but I knew that something was different, because, when Rev. James dipped me under the water, in the name of the Father, in the name of the Son and in the name of the Holy Ghost I remembered coming up and everybody looked different. I now know it was the presence of the Holy Spirit and I have never been the same.

I knew there was something different and as God used me to sing in the choir I felt empowered, I felt as though I was ministering. I sung for different programs at various churches, I spoke for Youth Day services and song the songs of Zion for my home church, and for different occasions at various churches. I knew there was something different, for I could feel something within and people would so often speak of the presence of God that they saw in me.

My prayer was always whether speaking or singing, "Lord, don't let them see me, but, Lord let them see and hear you". I would find myself awakening in the early morning hours with a song that wouldn't let me rest or being led to my Bible to read scriptures. HE always knew how to get my attention or to prepare me.

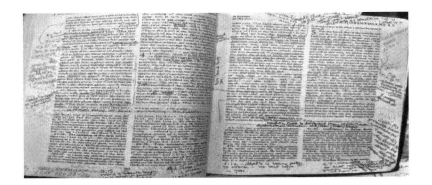

God Prepares You...

No matter where we meet God in life we have to know that our life prior was a preparation for servanthood. All of our life's experiences are the makeup of who we are. Those experiences can be used to enhance our lives as well as the lives of others, for now that we know better, we do better. We cannot profess to be His child and do as we did before we knew Him. For He tells us, I will not have you lukewarm. You're either cold or hot (meaning you are with God or you are not.) For if you are lukewarm I will spew you out (says the Lord), meaning He will have no part of you.

There were those who would say to me, you need to preach, God is doing something in your life, I can hear the anointing in your voice, when are you going to preach? I, too, knew there was a calling on my life, for I could feel the Holy

Spirit in my belly. It was as if I was trying to push something out, the depth and pressure was as if giving birth. I would find myself crying and saying no, Lord no, not me. HE continued to bless me, but HE also took from me. When life was taken from my (deceased) husband through Domestic Violence, I thought my world had come to an end.

When the reality of life sets in, and you find yourself at the brink of losing your mind, when you feel your HOPE is gone, when you're taken back and forth to the emergency room, when you feel you have to be strong in front of people, when you are advised and have to see a Psychiatrist, when you can hear your deceased husband saying, "be strong, you know I don't like a weak woman", when you need somebody to take the pain, take the hurt, to take the anger. When you can feel yourself leaving yourself, when pills and shots afford you no relief... oh, oh where is my God, where is He who I pray to, where is He who I live for, where is He who I witness about, where is HE?

You see, I didn't know what to do, what to expect in the future, how was I going to make it? Not so much financially, but, being without my helpmate. I tried so hard to bear my hurt, my disappointment, my not having an answer as to why, and all alone.

I felt so far from God, **but now** I know HE was closer than HE had ever been. I just needed to acknowledge HIS presence.

What had I done? What had I not done? I now know why I had song the song, "If the Lord need somebody, here am I Lord, I'll go", but had I really lived what I was singing? I knew HE had a higher calling upon my life, to not just sing, to not just speak on special occasions but to "preach"! To preach to dying men, women, boys and girls, that yes, Jesus does love you and to tell of HIS goodness and what HE can and will be in their lives. For I knew that "there is a fountain filled with blood, drawn from Emanuel's veins, and sinners plunge beneath the flood lose all their guilty stain".

I had thought of everything I could to make myself believe it was not God I was hearing but Satan was trying to mislead me. It wasn't so much of my feeling I wasn't being called but the feeling that I was not worthy…and then HE reminded me that I'm not worthy, but HIS grace, and HIS mercy has redeemed me and made it so.

Ephesians 2:8-9

[8] For it is by grace you have been saved, through faith—and this is not from

yourselves, it is the gift of God— [9] not by works, so that no one can boast.

Jesus, as we know, came to the people as He found they needed him. He came as a prophet. (Deuteronomy 18:14-22) He was a messenger sent by God, He was the Word of God in the flesh. Christ spoke for God to the people. And in Luke 4:24 he spoke of himself as a prophet when he said, "No prophet is accepted in his own native place". Are there times when you feel this way?

He was a priest. (Psalm 110:1-4) He offered his life for ours and now he sits on the right side of the Father making intercession for us. Doing what we are not able to do for ourselves.

He was called King of Kings. (Psalm 2) He was mocked, and he was arrested for being called a king. He didn't try to rule the people, but he served the people.

And so, what is your calling? Are you called to be a Prophet, an Apostle, a Pastor, a Teacher, Bishop or just a servant to mankind? Showing love and compassion to all you meet and through your life and actions leading them to a life of redemptive salvation…leading them to a belief and choice to serve a risen Savior.

In the midst of the Prophetic word, the answering to the call, I still found myself crying out to God. Crying out to God for I realized I needed HIM to do HIS work. I cried out to HIM saying, "Lord I need your Umption". The umption is when the Holy Spirit comes upon you. For Luke 4:18-19 tells us, the Spirit of the Lord is upon me – the umption. The Word tells us that after Jesus was baptized of his beloved son – the umption came upon him. Know that without the umption there is no power. The word says, you shall receive power after that the Holy Ghost has come upon you. The Holy

Spirit indwelling comes as a gift. It's the personal presence of God.

But don't get confused, the umption comes at a price. The cost is faithful prayer. You must know and recognize that to have a prayer life, you have to spend time with the Lord. You have to be willing to yield. Yield not to yourself, not to people, but **Yield to God** that you might do those things that are acceptable unto Him.

- God is able to do far more because He is omnipotent

- Pray big prayers with faith

- God is willing to do far beyond what we ask or think because He is God. Therefore, to God, we give all the glory, for truly He is worthy to be praised!

God Is Able…The Power of a Fervent Prayer

Ephesians 3:20-21

Now unto him that is able to do exceeding abundantly above all that we ask or think, according to the power that worketh in us,

Unto him be glory in the church by Christ Jesus throughout all ages, world without end. Amen.

Some of you may be feeling a little uncertainty, but the Great I Am says, to tell you, stop doubting, for "God Is Able", "God is Able"!

The Apostle Paul has just prayed that the Ephesians would be filled up to all the fullness of God. It's a prayer that they would come to total spiritual perfection! You can't go any higher than to be filled with all the fullness of God! But then Paul adds, "In case you think that it is too much to ask God to fill His saints to all of His fullness, remember that He is able to do far more abundantly beyond all that we ask or think, according to His power and for His glory." God IS ABLE

You see, some of us have been faced with cancer. Now, He didn't take the cancer, but he is allowing you to live a full life. You see he does not have to take or cure the illness, but He will sustain you. Your Drs. will look in awe, because you see, they gave up when they reached their limited gifts, and spoke closure on you and your life but... God Is Able.

Approximately 20 years ago my brother-in-law was diagnosed with a tumor near the brain stem. He was sent to the best of Dr.'s at Duke and they even referred him to the well-known Dr. Ben Carson for they said he was the only Dr. they knew who could perform the surgery. They, themselves would not chance it because it was too close to the brain stem. But, my brother-in-law reassured my sister, his wife, on that night not to worry, he would be alright. You see, he never lost his Hope, for He knew He trusted in and served a God who he (my brother-in-law) knew from the garden. You see, he had been going to the garden alone. He would go while the dew was still on the roses and the voice He'd hear, falling on his ear, He had learned that only the Son of God discloses. And he remembered, oh, how He'd walk with him, and how He would talk with him, and he didn't forget that He (God now) told him, he was his own. So, you see, he remembered,

GOD IS ABLE!

And today, approximately 20 years later, after being told by the top brain surgeon in the country, that he was afraid to bother the tumor because it was too close to the brain stem, but God, but God, my brother-in-law is a living testimony of God Is Able. He is a deacon in his church, he is a husband to his wife, he drives his car, drives to Indiana to see their daughter, would drive to Texas to see their son (when he lived there) now drives to Kernersville, NC to see the same son, mowers his grass, has a yard mowing business, cuts wood to sale during the winter months, tends a garden, and I could go on – God Is Able- and all this he does with the tumor still on his brain. You see, I've shared this to let us know that it's not about what we think or have even been told because God does not have to remove, nor does He have to heal, but He will sustain and keep you because it's about a God who is Able.

Oh, learn to pray a fervent prayer! It's about a God who is not just able to do beyond   what we ask, but abundantly beyond.

But that's not enough, He is able to do **far more abundantly** beyond what we ask. But, we still aren't to the limit: For the word says, "Now to Him who is able to do far more abundantly beyond all that we ask or think, according to the power that works within us." Now, what is it that you need? I want to encourage you to pray in faith, asking God to do far beyond all that you could ask or think.

Yet at the same time, I want to be realistic, for I know there are certain mysteries about the interaction between our prayers and the sovereign will of God that I cannot explain. When John the Baptist was imprisoned, I am sure that his disciples were praying for his release. It would have brought glory to God if John had been released to preach for many more years. Yet, John lost his head. Although God easily could have freed John (as He later freed Peter), it was not His will to do so.

When Jesus predicted Peter's denials, I would have thought that it would be right to pray that Peter not sin at all. But, Jesus didn't pray that. Rather, He prayed that after Peter had sinned and was restored, that he would strengthen his brothers (Luke 22:31-32). God's sovereign will permitted Peter's sin in order to strengthen Peter and others in the long run.

I am painfully aware of many situations where God has not answered my prayers. You see, for Him to do for His glory, is far more than I could ask or think. There have been lost people for whom I have prayed that they would be saved, but they were not saved. There have been broken Christian marriages that I have prayed would be restored, but they ended in divorce. There have been sinning Christians for whom I have prayed that they would repent, but there has been no repentance.

And so, I want to motivate you to pray big prayers with faith in a mighty God, who is able to do far more abundantly beyond all that we ask or think. And, yet at the same time, I don't want to gloss or mislead you over the difficult struggles that you will surely encounter in your prayer life. We simply cannot know the big picture of what God is doing, and so invariably we will experience disappointments in prayer.

SO, WHAT IS PRAYER?

Prayer is communicating with and hearing from God, but Jesus is our Mediator.

- God does not teach us the posture of prayer, because any posture will do.

People in the Bible prayed standing, lifting up their hands, sitting, lying down, kneeling, lifting their eyes toward Heaven, bowing, and crying out to Him in their own language.

- God does not teach us the place to pray, because any place will do.

- Jesus does not tell us when to pray, because any time will do.

No one is better qualified to teach us about how to pray than Jesus Himself. "Lord, teach us to pray" (Luke 11:1). The disciples brought this request to Jesus after they had witnessed the countless times He went out to spend time with His Father. And He taught them saying, "In this manner, therefore, pray:

Our Father which art in heaven, Hallowed be thy name.

Thy kingdom come, Thy will be done in earth, as it is in heaven.

Give us this day our daily bread.
And forgive us our debts, as we forgive our debtors.

And lead us not into temptation, but deliver us from evil: For thine is the kingdom, and the power, and the glory, for ever. Amen.
This model prayer, also called "The Lord's Prayer," covers every aspect of prayer. It can be divided into two parts.

The first three components of the prayer deal with God's glory: "Hallowed be Your name," "Your Kingdom come," and "Your will be done," while the second three components of the model prayer deal with our need. "Give us this day our daily bread," "Forgive us our debts," and "Lead us not into temptation." Yes, He taught us to have direct communication with Him.

Children of God keep on praying

Children of God keep on praying

Children of God keep on praying

One of these days you shall be free

Paul's prayer for God to do abundantly beyond what we ask, or think is not a prayer for physical miracles, but rather for Christ to dwell in the hearts of believers so that we may comprehend His great love for us, so that we will grow to complete spiritual maturity.

And so, because God is able to do far more abundantly beyond all that we ask or think, we should pray for that which would further His glory through Christ and His church.
So, God is saying:

Don't be guilty of not having because you haven't asked. God says (Psalm 81:10), "I, the Lord, am your God, who brought you up from the land of Egypt; open your mouth wide and I will fill it.

So, open wide! Ask! "GOD IS ABLE"

Don't be guilty of not having because you doubt God's ability or His willingness to give. Nothing is impossible with God! As the loving Father,

He will give good gifts to His children who ask (Matt. 7:11). We can't always understand His purposes, but we never should doubt His ability or His goodness towards us.

"GOD IS ABLE"

Don't be guilty of praying small prayers. Pray "big" prayers! It is impossible to ask God for too much, assuming that it is in line with His will and for His glory. So, children of the most High King, "Pray the largest prayers. You cannot think a prayer so large that God, in answering it, will not wish you had made it larger.

Pray, Pray large, Pray not for crutches but for wings."

So, pray for yourself but never cease to pray for your brothers and sisters. Pray for the renewing of the hearts and minds of sinners.

Pray for repentance and holiness for God's saints. Pray, yes pray that He will be glorified in your life and the lives of all generations forever and ever.

Let God meet you where you are...

God is able to save, to heal, to restore, to cleanse us of our sins.   God is able and will accept us just where we are, filthy- a wretch undone. God is Able, trust HIM, Believe Him for there is a fountain filled with blood, drawn from Emanuel's veins, and sinners plunge beneath the flood lose all their guilty stain.

God is Able, God is Able, God is Able! Trust Him, for God is Able!

Why not take the time to study PRAYER with me for 5 days! Yeah, the Power of Prayer.

Let's take a look at Nehemiah. You see, Nehemiah is a beautiful example of faith, prayer and action. In this study we will take a closer look at how Nehemiah approached God, and how we can use his example and apply it in our own lives. We will learn how effective prayer followed by action can change the world. We will look at three "types" of prayer. All forms of prayer are powerful. Each is a gift from the Lord with its own purpose.

The three types of prayer we will study are:

- PRAY - focused prayer time
- "Arrow" Prayers
- "Circle" Prayers

LET US HAVE A TALK WITH JESUS!

DAY ONE:

Let's begin by reading Nehemiah Chapter One. What news had Nehemiah just received from his brother and the other visitor's?

_____

_____

_____

_____

What was Nehemiah's reaction? How did he respond when he heard this news?

_____

_____

_____

_____

This is a wonderful transition into the first "type" prayer we will study. There is a fantastic model for prayer that we will reference throughout this study called the PRAY format. With the PRAY model you Praise, Repent,

Ask, and Yield. Read Chapter 1, verses 4-11 again. How does Nehemiah's response follow this model? Praise (thanking God, acknowledging who He is, reminding Him of His promises)

_____

_____

_____

_____

_____

_____

_____

Repent (Confess any sin in your life, be honest with God, ask for and receive forgiveness)

_____

_____

_____

_____

_____

_____

_____

Ask (Tell God what you need, enjoy the ability to approach the thrown of grace)

_____

_____

_____

_____

_____

_____

_____

Yield (Surrender yourself to God)

_____

_____

_____

_____

_____

_____

_____

From the very First Chapter of Nehemiah, he offers us a beautiful example of **effective prayer**. We can use this example as we approach the Lord in prayer. This example of prayer is not only powerful in response to difficult news or situations, but in every facet of our prayer life. In this study we will use his example to provide a model for our own "prayer plan". Read Chapter two. Why was Nehemiah sad and deeply troubled?

_____

_____

_____

_____

It was dangerous for Nehemiah to allow the King to see him struggle. At best, an indication of mourning or sadness could get you banned from the palace. At worst, it could be a death sentence. The King could execute anyone who displeased him for any reason. Read and underline in your Bible the first three words of Chapter Two, verse three. Write it below:

_____

_____

_____

_____

Why is this response so important?

_____

_____

_____

_____

_____

_____

_____

_____

_____

_____

_____

Nehemiah was "badly frightened". Fear can be a powerful influence, can't it? Battling fear is something most of us are well acquainted with. Fear has been a stronghold in most our lives for as long as we can remember. As I walk my walk with Christ, I continue to have to actively fight against fear. If fear is a stronghold in your life, I assure you I understand.

Nehemiah's life is an amazing encouragement to us in that way! Nehemiah had very good reason to feel frightened. His life was literally on the line. He didn't let that fear paralyze him though. He could have, no one would have blamed him – but he didn't. Verse three tells us he was scared, BUT HE REPLIED. He refused to let fear stop Him from what He knew God was calling him to do. If fear tends to hold you back, remember that God is infinitely more powerful than fear.

He will never, no NEVER forsake you or leave you without His power and strength. Speaking the Word of God is the most powerful tool to break fear's hold on you.

DAY TWO:

What Nehemiah does next is an important place for us to meditate for a minute. Carefully read Nehemiah 2:4-5. Before he responded to the King, what did Nehemiah do?

_____

_____

_____

This short little sentence is so important. It's important because it tells us something about how Nehemiah approached prayer and brings us to the second "form" of prayer we'll study – **arrow prayers**. The Lord gives us arrow prayers for those moments when we need quick and powerful help. Help with words, instant decisions, emergency situations, even praise and worship.

They are the on-the-spot, anytime-anywhere type of prayers. Notice that he didn't ask the

King for time to go away and pray about his response. He didn't put off answering until he'd scheduled an hour of uninterrupted time in his prayer closet. Those are AN approach to prayer, but notice that in this situation, Nehemiah didn't have the luxury of time to think or plan. His INSTANT response was prayer - quick, direct, immediate prayer. These kinds of prayers are sometimes referred to as "arrow" prayers. Just a quick shot straight to the heart of the Father. This is so important because I've heard believers say time and time again that their prayer lives fall short because they can't seem to find time to really focus on it, or set aside quiet time with the Lord.

While it is of course important to spend focused quiet time with God, this example is critically important for us to grasp because it was clearly powerful in the life of Nehemiah.

When he needed help his MO was to quickly, directly, immediately consult God.

In fact, eight times in this short book we see Nehemiah "spontaneously" pray. Nehemiah provides such a wonderful example of this as we see him over and over again quickly seeking the Lord in prayer AND THEN replying.

Now look at 1 Thessalonians 5:16-18, and after reading, fill in the blank: "Always be joyful. _____ _____

_____.

Be thankful in all circumstances, for this is God's will for you who belong to Christ Jesus." I reference this passage because I firmly believe the Father heart of God desires prayer as an ongoing conversation with us. Not perfectly planned fancy words. The kind of prayer I believe God desires are, I imagine, the same kind of conversation you'd have with your mom, sister, husband, or best friend.

I believe from the depth of my soul that God the FATHER, our Daddy, our friend, the lover of our souls wants to talk with us about EVERYTHING! If He knows the number of hairs on my head, why wouldn't He want me to talk to Him about them when I discover they're falling out and I have no answer as to why? I think he's ok with me asking for instructional care. Remember, I was made by Him! I feel very confident encouraging you to do it, don't believe the lying whispers that something isn't worthy of God's time or attention. That's the voice of the Enemy, it's not God telling you that.

Reading Nehemiah 2:8, the King granted Nehemiah's request. According to Nehemiah, why?

_____

_____

_____

_____

_____

Our words aren't what make prayer powerful, it's the Receiver Who makes them powerful. The Lord calls us to the work, plans and purposes He desires for our lives and it's by His strength, power, and might that we accomplish more than we may even dare dream or imagine!

DAY THREE:

Read Nehemiah 2:11-20. This portion of scripture provides a perfect introduction to our third method of prayer – **circle prayers**.

Will you draw a prayer circle around your own prayers and refuse to budge from your commitment to pray them? I encourage you to unleash your God-given dreams and desires to prayer. I'm talking outrageously, audaciously, ridiculously huge prayers – the kind that God alone can and delights in answering.

Of course, there is nothing inherently "magical" about the act of drawing circles around your prayers, but it is a practical, visual, tangible way to help us focus with intensity on our prayers. Nehemiah had a circle prayer. Based on Nehemiah 2:11-20, how would you describe his "circle prayer" –

the kind of audacious, god-sized prayer only
God could answer?

_____

_____

_____

_____

_____

_____

_____

_____

_____

_____

_____

_____

_____

_____

_____

_____

_____

_____

_____

Nehemiah was bold. He had a bold vision. He had plans he'd dreamed up with God and he was pumped up about them! Like Nehemiah, when we are bold our prayers can change the world. God puts dreams and visions in your heart. With Him, even the most unthinkable, outrageous, out of this world huge dreams and ideas imaginable are possible. And, in fact, He probably has infinitely more in mind! Nothing, NOTHING is too huge for God. When God directs our paths, nothing is impossible. In the words of Nehemiah, the God of heaven will help you succeed!

When we offer a circle prayer to the Lord we are committing to the steadfast belief that He is capable of answering them. This is the kind of prayer that simply CANNOT happen without

God, it HAS to be Him, or it may actually be impossible. A circle prayer is one you offer to the Lord until He answers, you commit to it, you don't give up on it. Flip back in your Bible to Joshua Chapter Six. Read Joshua 6:1-20. There is no "right" answer here, what reasons can you think of for God's approach? Why do you think He approached the battle the way He did?

_____

_____

_____

_____

_____

_____

_____

_____

_____

_____

_____

_____

_____

_____

_____

_____

Imagine for a moment that Joshua gave up. What if on day five he thought "I'm tired, let's just bag this thing." Or, what if they stopped praying on day six, one day short of the miracle? What if we are supposed to march for another day? What if that prayer you've been praying is just one day from the miracle? What if we stop asking too soon and miss the miracle because we gave up and left the circle? A circle prayer is not a threat, it's not a test, it's not looking to God to be an answer vending machine. A circle prayer IS a faith-building, relationship strengthening opportunity to give the Lord unreal, HUGE glory.

You'll find that "God honors bold prayers because bold prayers honor God." Why not take this time write out three bold prayers. They can be individual, for family, business, community, even the world. Will you dare to allow God to reveal His hugest dreams for you? Will you have the courage to ask God to plant an idea or vision in you that will accomplish for Him more than you can even dare dream or imagine? Then, trust the Holy Spirit to get to work and pray it until God accomplishes it? Make sure you include the date, so you can look back and praise God, these serve as huge faith milestones!

_____

_____

_____

_____

_____

_____

_____

_____

_____

_____

_____

DAY FOUR:

As we look at the second half of Nehemiah we
begin to understand another element of an
effective prayer life. Let's go to the New
Testament and read Matthew 7:7, write it out
here:

_____

_____

_____

_____

_____

_____

_____

_____

_____

_____

Do you notice that there is an element of
persistence and action in this verse? There is

SO much packed into this single verse. The gist of the verse though is this: Pray. Then, pray some more. Pray often. Pray hard. Pray with endurance. Then, after you've prayed, move. Take action. Rarely do we open a door for no reason, it's usually so someone can walk through it. A door is opened to allow movement to take place. With this in mind, lets now read Nehemiah 4:9-23. Nehemiah was persistent. He was consistent. He had amazing follow through. The truth is that accomplishing any significant project, plan or task is hard. It's tiring. There are obstacles and discouragements. It takes only the kind of strength and endurance God can offer. Again, read Nehemiah 4:10-14, what did Nehemiah do to keep the people motivated?

_____

_____

_____

_____

_____

_____

Keeping our minds on the eternal goal is the cure for discouragement every time. It's for this reason that having a very clear, very defined "why" is so important.

When we set out in prayer to accomplish something for the Lord, we must have a "why" He can work with. You see, we must know that one of the most important things we can do is declare a "why" that has eternal meaning. In weight loss, if our why is to simply look better, wear smaller pants, get more attention, even be more confident, we are vulnerable. Those are pretty situational motives and can vary from day to day. However, we determine to live at our best weight, in our strongest, most effective bodies to be effective for the Lord's purposes, clothed in holiness (not a certain size), all to draw people to Him so they can discover freedom. If our motivation is to be energetic and enjoy with vigor, what we are called to do we will never be let down. When you feel tempted to throw in the towel, call upon Nehemiah's prayer.

Read Nehemiah 6:9, what did Nehemiah pray for?

_____

_____

_____

DAY FIVE:

When we pray, and our hearts and prayers are aligned with that of the Father (this is why it's important to know the character of God and His word), we can rest in knowing that He is at work. Sometimes His timing is different than we'd choose, but if there's a chance for Him to get glory and draw more of His kids to Him, you can believe with steadfast assurance that your prayers will not go unheard. Like His timing, sometimes His answers are different than we might think.

There may be opposition, there may be obstacles, there may be enormous patience needed. The greater the prayer, the greater the glory and as we've already read, God LOVES to answer those kinds of prayers. Nehemiah 6:15 is so incredibly powerful and encouraging! According to the verse, how was their work accomplished?

_____

_____

This verse also teaches us another very important example to apply to our own lives. When they accomplished all that they'd set out to (with God's blessing) and He responded faithfully, what did they do?

_____

_____

_____

_____

_____

_____

Recording answered prayers in writing is such a powerful tool to help keep the faith.

Recording times when God was faithful to answer your prayers allows you to look back and recall His faithfulness during times when doubt creeps in. Make sure to include important scriptures the Lord spoke or used during that time, dates, and other milestone moments. I jot down notes in my bible and use a memory log to write down answered prayers. Nehemiah's life of prayerfulness, perseverance, faithfulness, integrity and leadership provide an amazing example for us to apply to our own lives.

Above all, what we take from the life of Nehemiah is this – keep your sights on God. Talk with Him constantly. Don't let the cares of the world pull your attention away from Him. And, don't forget to thank Him for His answers. When we do this, truly, truly anything is possible!

As we come to the end our 5- day PRAYER time with God, let each of us remember just how amazing prayer is. We now know that because of our communicating with Him, we have a peace that we can and should talk to Him about everything. We have the courage to pray huge, bold, outrageously audacious prayers to give Him glory! So, with gracious thanksgiving, we thank you Lord for teaching us how to be as close to you as possible.

Thank you for showing us how to use the power of prayer. Thank you for the strength to be persistent, to push through obstacles and opposition. Lord, we are ready to be used by you! May the name of Jesus be exalted as we work wonders through our prayers! We praise you, we pray to you and we seek answers in Jesus name, Amen!

Calvary Covered It All...

The death of Jesus on the cross was the greatest and most important event the world will ever see. For at Calvary, on the cross, Atonement was made for our sins. In the garden, God told Adam that he could eat freely from the fruit of every tree, "but of the tree of the knowledge of good and evil you shall not eat, for in the day that you eat of it you shall surely die" (Genesis 2:17). Adam ate of that tree, and he died. He began to die physically that day, but more importantly, he died spiritually. His sin caused a separation between himself and God (Isaiah 59:1-2). He needed to make atonement for this sin, but was powerless to do so. Therefore, man needed to be redeemed!

Death was the penalty for sin. That was the price that had to be paid. The Law of Moses called for the sacrifice of bulls and goats. Their life was given, and their blood was shed, but to no effect, "For it is not possible that the blood of bulls and goats could take away sins" (Hebrew 10:4). It couldn't be just any death. It was a man's soul that was lost in the garden, atonement required a man's death. But, it couldn't be just any man. A sinless soul was lost in Eden, so, only a sinless man could make atonement.

Thus, the perfect Son of God had to die. "For He made Him who knew no sin to be sin for us, that we might become the righteousness of

God in Him" (2 Corinthians 5:21). Only in the death of Jesus is this wrong made right and God's righteous judgment satisfied. In the cross we see the painful reality of what has been said, **"He paid a debt He didn't owe because we owed a debt we couldn't pay."**

At Calvary, prophecies were fulfilled. Our Lord's death on the cross was no accident. It was planned in the mind of God before time began (Acts 2:23). It was foretold to the world through the prophets.

- The suffering servant of Isaiah 53
- the pierced hands and feet of Psalm 22
- no broken bones of Psalm 34
- given gall and vinegar in Psalm 69
- and beaten and spat upon in Isaiah 50.

All of these pointed to Calvary.

You see, at Calvary, the Old Law was put

away. "And me, being dead in my trespasses and the uncircumcision of my flesh, He has made alive together with Him, having forgiven me of all my trespasses, having wiped out the handwriting of requirements that was against me, which was contrary to me. And He has taken it out of the way, for it was nailed to the cross" (Colossians 2:13-14). That old law was nailed to the cross with Jesus. When He died, the veil of the temple was torn in two (Matthew 27:51), signifying the end of the law it represented.

The law of Moses was taken out of the way. God said it would be: "Behold, the days are coming, says the Lord, when I will make a new covenant with the house of Israel and with the house of Judah - not according to the covenant that I made with their fathers in the day when I took them by the hand to lead them out of the land of Egypt; because they did not continue in My covenant, and I disregarded them, says the Lord" (Hebrew 8:8-9).

We now live under the law of Christ (Galatians 6:2). We don't live under a combination of the law of Moses and the law of Christ, but we are living under a new and better covenant.

So now we ask the question, why should there be Enmity? Why should there be hate, why should there be hostility? For Enmity was abolished. "For He Himself is our peace, who has made both one, and has broken down the middle wall of separation, having abolished in His flesh the enmity, that is, the law of commandments contained in ordinances, so as to create in Himself one new man from the two, thus making peace, and that He might reconcile them both to God in one body through the cross, thereby putting to death the enmity"

(Ephesians 2:14-16). The law that separated the Jew from Gentile is gone. The gospel truly is for all. "Then Peter opened his mouth and said: 'In truth I perceive that God shows no partiality. But in every nation whoever fears Him and works righteousness is accepted by Him'" (Acts 10:34-35).

And yes, God demonstrates His own love toward us, in that while we were still sinners, Christ died for us" (Romans 5:8). Could God have done any better? What more could He have done? Jesus said, "Greater love has no one than this, than to lay down one's life for his friends" (John 15:13). Hours after He said this, He did it. He laid down His life for His friends, His enemies, you and me. If you ever begin to doubt God's love for you, ever wonder if He really knows and cares about you, remember the cross. There has never been a greater act of love.

Perhaps you have read the following before: "I asked Jesus how much He loved Me. 'This much,' He answered, then stretched out His arms and died." He was a perfect example in suffering. Times of suffering are going to come to all of us. We will all face trials various times in our lives. How can we make it through it? Jesus' death on the cross left us both encouragement and an example. "For to this you were called, because Christ also suffered for us, leaving us an example, that you should follow His steps: Who committed no sin, nor was deceit found in His mouth; who, when He was reviled, did not revile in return; when He suffered, He did not threaten, but committed Himself to Him who judges righteously; who Himself bore our sins in His own body on the tree, that we, having died to sins, might live for righteousness - by whose stripes you were healed" (1 Peter 2:21-24).

Jesus' death on the cross not only paid the penalty for our sin, it also showed us that we can endure any suffering that we have to face. If Jesus can endure the cross for us, then we can endure anything for Him.

I am troubled yet not distressed

Perplexed but not in despair

I'm a vessel full of power

With a treasure non can compare

Thank you lord   Jesus

Persecuted but not forsaken

Cast down but not destroyed

I am a vessel full of holy ghost power

I've got a treasure from the lord

Bruised and battered but not broken

Born in sin but from sin set free

I'm a vessel full of holy ghost power

I've got a treasure hidden in me

Thank you, Father for your power

It has resurrected me

Oh, the painful God knows I've had some I've had some painful circumstances that my poor soul could not flee

Thank you, Father for your power

It has resurrected me

Oh, the painful circumstances

that my poor soul could not flee

(Kathy Taylor- "Corinthian Song" at Mt Zion Nashville YouTube)

When life is no more as you knew it…

There's an ole saying that "death comes in three's". Death, it's presence is never the same. It comes with mixed feelings and emotions. It comes with unanswered questions and will make you question your FAITH. And that is where I found myself approximately 1 year and 4 months after losing my mom and having to experience the devastation of losing my husband.

I looked at my siblings, standing around his bedside and waited for the true reality to set in. Death had done it again, to me, why me? And I received my answer in the form of a question, why not? The Lord giveth, and the Lord taketh, blessed be the name of the Lord. Job 1:21 And again, HE granted me a peace that surpassed my own understanding.

Sometime later, in the midst of dealing with and accepting my grief, and having accepted my calling, I was led to go to the nursing facility to see Pastor (Apostle Mary Phillips). I went expecting to see her in bed but witnessed the complete opposite.

She was sitting up in the chair and her face just lit up when she saw me. My heart was full of so much joy and thanksgiving- it made my day. My sister-in-law (Pastor, Evangelist Annie Howard), and Apostle Phillip's grandson were in the room. To be a witness to how frail her man-spirit was, yet her spirit man was sooooo strong. She told us to be good. She told us to be good to Donnie(Apostle) to do what he tells us. I asked her if she wanted to sing a song, she said yes. I song "Yes Jesus loves me". She relaxed, closed her eyes and would open her eyes, look at me, smile, and seemingly allow her spirit man to take her somewhere else.

When I finished the song, she said, you look good. I told her, "you look good too". She said, you look good, be good. Then she said, "you blessed, write". My sister-in-law immediately said, I told you – that's your confirmation.

You have to know that the words "you look good", she was not seeing me physically, but spiritually. When the "spirits" touch and agree, there is a revelation- the anointing fails not.

1Corinthians 6:19 - What? know ye not that your body is the temple of the Holy Ghost [which is] in you, which ye have of God, and ye are not your own?

Because of her mental state, she conversed but we were not always able to understand but when the prophetic word came, it was spoken with clarity.

John 14:26 - But the Comforter, [which is] the Holy Ghost, whom the Father will send in my name, he shall teach you all things, and bring all things to your remembrance, whatsoever I have said unto you.

Every visit with her, I would leave more empowered and on a quest to get closer to my Savior.

On this day, God allowed me to see that my life truly is not about me. It's all about HIM and HIS

PURPOSE for my life. That just as the word says, "night will come when no man can work" – our night is when our earthly tabernacle, our bodies can no longer function as we knew it but the joy is knowing that when "our night" comes, if we have accepted Jesus as our personal Savior, then the HOLY SPIRIT, our SPIRIT MAN takes control and will touch and agree with other's spirit man that God might get the glory until HE says "well done" and receives our "spirit man' unto Himself!

John 9:4

I must work the works of him that sent me, while it is day: the night cometh, when no man can wor

k.

My Soul Cries Out…

(my feeling Gods call upon my life, feeling unworthy- I accepted, and HE sent the comforter to abide within that I might recognize, hear and obey; I accepted my calling.)

> The Spirit of the Lord is upon me,
> because he has anointed me
> to bring glad tidings to the
> poor. Luke 4:18

I've learned that according to the New Testament every Christian is called to dedicate their life to God. As such, every believer must be ready and willing to take his cross and follow the Lord in daily faithfulness and service. Therefore, every Christian should present himself to God as a living sacrifice and dedicate their life fully to the will of God. That entails obedience and that I had not been.

Yes, God has a way of getting your attention. I found myself on my back porch fussing out my (deceased) husband and my God. The God I professed to love and knew HE loved me. I asked HIM why and I recall hearing that still, small voice say, "Because HE had something better for you". Don't be misled, my deceased husband was a good man, he loved me, had been a husband, he was good to me. But what I've learned is that in your relationship with God comes understanding.

You see when HE said something better, He wasn't referring to "man" but to the Spirit. For He was about to take me on a long-awaited mission. A mission to serve Him and His people. The something better was my "calling" to preach the word, to be instant in season, to preach the word out of season, to preach the word when men would hear me, to preach the word when men would not her me, to preach the word…that was my "something better"!

So, you have to understand that everything that God made was good and very good, so if He was giving back to me, why would He (my God), my Heavenly Father) give me less?… and at the same time, I could feel myself leaving myself. But GOD…I felt myself leaving myself, could not save myself…But GOD…I heard my phone ring, I answered it and I heard the voice of my friend (Katrina) say, "Gwen as close as you are to God you know HE has not forgotten you"…that was when I acknowledged HE was with me and I knew in my spirit HE had a work for me to do.

God, will not only give you what you want but what you need.

Psalms 37:4 "Delight thyself also in the Lord; and he shall give thee the desires of thine heart."

Approximately 3 days later, HE brought Jessie Bowen into my life at Beauty World, after I had attended a funeral in Rocky Mount. I had not been in a church in approximately seven months after my (deceased) husband's death. HE gave me my helpmate back. Jessie is my friend, my psychologist, my confidant but most of all my partner in my walk with Christ. Oh, what a mighty God I serve!

A Charge To Women

Dare you not step out, woman of valor?

Mother, wife, homemaker, counselor, compassionate listener, vision seeker, hope finder, friend, companion, defender of the brethren, angel of mercy, pillar of grace, trusted of God, moving spirit

Dare you not step out? Dare you not step out?

Did the Lord not choose you to be a woman of authority, the carrier of the seed?

Let us arise and go forth, for we are armed with the Strength of The Almighty.

Faith in God and what He can do, is our sound foundation as we proclaim to the world.

"Is not the Lord gone out before thee"?

(Poem written to and for me by Sister Faye Howard – Oak Grove Christian Church Greenville, N.C.)

During a service at Oak Grove Church on May 11, 2016, the Prophet for the service called me out. He stated that I was being called into the ministry. It was at that moment that I openly shared that I was being called of God to preach and I accepted my calling. What a relief...I felt so good...I was able to rejoice and share with my husband upon returning home. My husband rejoiced with me and to hear him say he would be there as my support person meant so much. I am not only thankful but grateful that God loved me so much that HE would assign me such a task.

Staying prayerful, I am excited about learning more about God that I might do as Ephesians 6:11-18 says:

[11] Put on the whole armour of God, that ye may be able to stand against the wiles of the devil.

12 For we wrestle not against flesh and blood, but against principalities, against powers, against the rulers of the darkness of this world, against spiritual wickedness in high places.

13 Wherefore take unto you the whole armour of God, that ye may be able to withstand in the evil day, and having done all, to stand.

14 Stand therefore, having your loins girt about with truth, and having on the breastplate of righteousness;

15 And your feet shod with the preparation of the gospel of peace;

16 Above all, taking the shield of faith, wherewith ye shall be able to quench all the fiery darts of the wicked.

17 And take the helmet of salvation, and the sword of the Spirit, which is the word of God:

[18] Praying always with all prayer and supplication in the Spirit, and watching thereunto with all perseverance and supplication for all saints;

Here Am I Lord, Use Me!

My prayer for you is that you will allow God to meet you just where you are. Study His Word. Get to know who He is, but don't keep the Good News to yourself. As He

reveals Himself to you, share with someone. Pray, communicate with Him and be a living testimony of His goodness. Let it be known that I am not ashamed of the gospel, for

MY SOUL CRIES OUT!

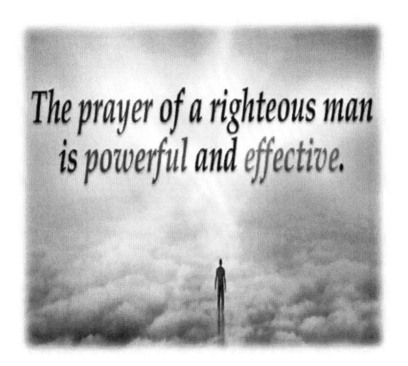

The prayer of a righteous man is powerful and effective.

Refer to these scriptures as you

PRAY WITHOUT CEASING

- The prayer of a righteous man availeth much. James 5:16

- This is the confidence we have in approaching God: that if we ask anything according to His will, He hears us. 1 John 5:14

- If my people, who are called by my name, will humble themselves and pray and seek my face and turn from their wicked ways, then I will hear from heaven, and I will forgive their sin and will heal their land. 2 Chronicles 7:14

- I pray that the eyes of your heart may be enlightened in order that you may know the hope to which he has called you, the riches of his glorious inheritance in His holy people Ephesians 1:18

- And pray in the Spirit on all occasions with all kinds of prayers and requests. With this in mind, be alert and always keep on praying for all the Lord's people. Ephesians 6:18

- Therefore, I tell you, whatever you ask for in prayer, believe that you have received it, and it will be yours. Mark 11:24

- And when you pray, do not keep on babbling like pagans, for they think they will be heard because of their many words. Mark 6:7

- I call on you, my God, for you will answer me; turn your ear to me and hear my prayer.   Psalm 17:6

- May my prayer be set before you like incense; may the lifting up of my hands be like the evening sacrifice.   Psalm 141:2

- Do not conform to the pattern of this world, but be transformed by the renewing of your mind. Then you will be able to test and approve what God's will is—His good, pleasing and perfect will. Romans 12:2

Notes

Notes

Notes

Notes

Notes

Notes

Notes

Notes

Notes

Notes

Notes

Made in the USA
Columbia, SC
25 April 2019